THE MIND AND YOUR CHRISTIAN WALK

THE IMPACT OF THE MIND ON OUR CHRISTIAN WALK

BISI OLADIPUPO

SPRINGS OF LIFE PUBLISHING

DEDICATION

To Jesus Christ, my Lord and Saviour—to Him alone that laid down His life that l might have life eternal. To Him that led
captivity captive and gave gifts unto men (Ephesians 4:8). One of those gifts is writing!

Bisi Oladipupo

CONTENTS

Foreword — VII

Introduction — IX

1. Your mind can reason you out! — 1

2. It takes a renewed mind to discern God's Will — 3

3. Being Spiritually minded — 6

4. Your mind and your prayer life — 9

5. Your Mind and Praying in the Spirit — 11

6. Your mind and your affections — 13

7. Sharing our faith — 15

8. The Mind of Christ — 16

9. Being Sober-Minded — 18

10. A Focused Mind — 20

11. The Cost of being carnally minded — 21

12. Conclusion — 23

Salvation Prayer — 24

About The Author 25

Also By Bisi 27

FOREWORD

The Scripture says that knowledge shall increase in the end times (Daniel 12:4).

Depending on when and how you became a Christian, the importance our minds play in our Christian walk may not have yet dawned on you.

Did you know that if not put in check and the instructions of the Bible are not applied to our minds, our minds can actually hinder our Christian walk?

According to Scripture, we are made up of three parts: spirit, soul, and body (1 Thessalonians 5:23).

Our souls consist of our will, mind, and emotions, and there is a reason the Bible instructs and tells us what to think about (Philippians 4:8-9).

It is possible to be hindered in our Christian walk if we do not obey the instructions on what to do with our minds.

This book will look at the many instructions of what the Bible tells us to do with our minds.

For some, it confirms what they already know, while for others, it will enlighten them on why certain struggles have persisted.

Above all, my prayer is that the Holy Spirit will breathe upon the pages of this book so that each reader will receive something that they can apply to their Christian walk.

Bisi Oladipupo

INTRODUCTION

S o, why the mind?

To live successful Christian lives, we need to realise that the three parts are inclusive of this journey: our spirit, soul, and body made up the being called man (1 Thessalonians 5:23).

God is a Spirit, so we contact God with our spirits (Romans 1:9).

God is a Spirit: and they that worship him must worship him in spirit and in truth (John 4:24).

Once we make Jesus Christ the Lord of our lives, our spirits are made alive unto God (Romans 8:10), and we are already in the Spirit (Romans 8:9).

We then need to build up ourselves and feed on the Word of God.

As for our bodies, it must be disciplined. We cannot allow our bodies to do what it wants to do. Paul puts it this way, "I bring my body under" (1 Corinthians 9:27). We also need to take care of our bodies (1 Corinthians 6:20).

Now, we need to speak about the soul. The soul is the mind, will, and emotions. The scriptures tell us what we need to do about our souls.

The Lord wants our souls to prosper (3 John 2), which according to scripture, can impact our health. Our souls also need to be saved. *But I thought I got saved when I received Jesus Christ as my Lord and Saviour?* Yes, we did get saved; however, only our spirits were changed and made a new creation. The spirit is the inner man, while the outward man is the body (2 Corinthians 4:16).

Here is what the Bible says about our souls:

Wherefore lay apart all filthiness and superfluity of naughtiness, and **receive with meekness the engrafted word, which is able to save your souls** (James 1:21).

If you notice, the Bible says that God's Word is able to save our souls. In other words, we must allow God's Word to save our souls.

Receiving the end of your faith, even the salvation of your souls (1 Peter 1:9).

For the purpose of this book, we are looking only at the mind.

CHAPTER ONE

YOUR MIND CAN REASON YOU OUT!

Did you know that if allowed, your mind can reason you out? Your mind can say, "No, we are not doing it that way".

This is what happened to the woman in the garden known as Eve. God had already told them not to eat the tree of the knowledge of good and evil. However, Eve was deceived by the serpent, and she allowed her reasoning, her mind to talk her out of God's will, which impacted all mankind.

And when the woman saw that the tree was good for food, and that it was pleasant to the eyes, and a tree to be desired to make one wise, she took of the fruit thereof, and did eat, and gave also unto her husband with her; and he did eat (Genesis 3:6).

The reasoning would have taken place in her mind, and she missed God.

Before we start throwing stones at Eve, we all have been victims of wrong choices due to our minds telling us things contrary to the right choice. What we have to realise is that our minds are limited. The natural mind will only go by what it sees, smells, and hears. Therefore, we must know God's word and be led by the Spirit of God (Romans 8:14). We must make decisions and allow truth to lead us. God's word is truth and whatever the

Holy Spirit tells us to do in that situation is truth (John 16: 13).). This is what should always prevail in any decision that we take. All we need to see is what happened to Eve and how her natural reasoning caused her to miss God.

Chapter Two

IT TAKES A RENEWED MIND TO DISCERN GOD'S WILL

S ometimes we forget that we are threefold. This has already been explained in an earlier chapter.

Prayer has a great role to play in our Christian walk. In fact, people that don't know the Lord, even pray. Everyone will pray when the rubber hits the road, but as Christians, it does not stop at praying. We must renew our minds; it is a necessity.

And be not conformed to this world: but be ye transformed by the renewing of your mind, that ye may prove what is that good, and acceptable, and perfect, will of God (Romans 12:2).

From the above scripture, how do we prove God's will? By renewing our minds.

We renew our minds by the Word of God.

This explains why many have been praying and not seeing results. It's not enough to pray; we need to align our thinking with God's Word. Why is this important? Because after you pray, if a person's thinking has not been renewed and aligned to God's Word and His ways, even when the answer comes, it could easily be aborted. This is because a wrong mindset, which is unrenewed in God's Word and ways, can easily choose what is not of God. Such a person might not have the discernment to accept God's remedy or answer to the request.

That ye put off concerning the former conversation the old man, which is corrupt according to the deceitful lusts; **And be renewed in the spirit of your mind**; *And that ye put on the new man, which after God is created in righteousness and true holiness. Wherefore putting away lying, speak every man truth with his neighbour: for we are members one of another. Be ye angry, and sin not: let not the sun go down upon your wrath: Neither give place to the devil* (Ephesians 4:22-27).

If you look at the above scriptures, we are told to put off certain things and put on some stuff. This is all part of renewing our minds. Verse 23 summarises this, **"And be renewed in the spirit of your mind".**

The scriptures here instruct us to put away the old man and tell us to speak the truth. Speaking the truth is part of putting on the new man. Our new man has been created after God, that is, our spirits. Now, our souls need to put that on, too. This is the process of renewing our minds to what we already are in our spirits.

In every situation, truth is always God's way—that is an example of how a renewed mind would respond to any situation.

So, when you get into any situation, remind yourself that you are created in righteousness and true holiness, then respond accordingly.

I remember wanting to stop a cheque many years ago when they were still in use. So, l called the bank and explained that l wanted to stop a cheque. The customer service rep then explained the charges and said that if l stopped the cheque, there would be a charge, but there would be no charge if l lost the cheque. For some reason, the bank staff went over the two options again. So, l told the bank staff that l did not lose the cheque but wanted to stop the cheque. So, l got charged, which was fine by me.

That is an example of how we find ourselves sometimes in some situations, but we must speak the truth at all times. We must be people of integrity always.

CHAPTER THREE

BEING SPIRITUALLY MINDED

The scriptures tell us that being spiritually minded is life and peace.

For to be carnally minded is death; but to be spiritually minded is life and peace (Romans 8:6).

So, what does it mean to be spiritually minded? It simply means to set one's mind on the things of the Spirit. Make decisions after the Spirit, i.e., to be focused on the things of the Spirit. And in this case, being spiritually minded is being focused on God's things—making decisions after the ways of God and His Word. This will make a huge difference in the way we live our lives. Instead of getting into an argument, allow your mind to respond in the way the Lord asks us to respond. This will result in peace instead of a long-winded argument.

Have you ever seen a great giant of faith and wondered how they live? It is because they have chosen to focus their minds on spiritual matters, on the things of God.

We live in a world where if you are not intentional, you can leave your Christianity after your quiet time in the morning, and for the rest of the day, live like a natural person. As Christians, we live in two worlds, and we need to be aware of that all the time.

A spiritually-minded person is always aware of God's presence, focusing their minds on things above. *God, what are you saying? What do you want me to say to this lady at the supermarket?* I think it is safe to say that many believers do not walk in the supernatural on a daily basis because we simply do not focus our minds on it.

Set your affection on things above, not on things on the earth (Colossians 3:2).

Set your mind on things above, not on things on the earth" (Colossians 3:2; NKJV)

We need to be intentional about setting our minds on the things above. This is part of being sober-minded (Titus 2:6). For example, if you had to set your alarm clock to a particular time to wake you up, you would intentionally set your clock to the time you want to wake up. This is how we need to set our minds on the things above. This is an intentional step; it won't just happen. We must be intentional.

Being spiritually minded will also help us have a healthier and better perspective about issues that could weigh a person down. Casting our cares upon the Lord is part of being spiritually-minded. This would allow the peace of God to guide our hearts and minds through Christ Jesus.

*Be careful for nothing; but in every thing by prayer and supplication with thanksgiving let your requests be made known unto God. And the peace of God, which passeth all understanding, **shall keep your hearts and minds through Christ Jesus*** (Philippians 4:8).

This is why you can find a person going through a difficult time yet be at great peace. One reason is that the person has decided to be spiritually minded about the matter.

I remember meeting a lady that had just lost her brother a few years ago. She was happy and relaxed. If you didn't ask her, you would have never known that something like that had at that time recently happened to her. When she ended up sharing what happened, she said something to the effect that "I know where my brother is". He was a believer, and she chose to be spiritually minded about it. I know that it also takes the comfort of the Holy Spirit, but l was really amazed at the composition after such an incident.

Thou wilt keep him in perfect peace, whose mind is stayed on thee: because he trusteth in thee (Isaiah 26:3).

CHAPTER FOUR

YOUR MIND AND YOUR PRAYER LIFE

We have seen from the Book of Romans chapter 8 that to be spiritually minded is life and peace.

For to be carnally minded is death; but to be spiritually minded is life and peace (Romans 8:6).

We need to apply this to our prayer lives since it is now obvious that being spiritually minded is life and peace.

Did you know that if permitted, your mind can hinder your prayer life? You want to pray, and then, suddenly, thoughts start flooding your mind. You think about the food you left in the oven; something you forgot to do springs suddenly to mind.

A practical way to get the mind quiet is to have a journal or diary near you and just write anything that comes to mind. Then, those things can be dealt with later.

You will also need to bring every thought captive to the obedience of Christ (2 Corinthians 10:5). You will need to be intentional about staying your mind on the Lord. Many have said that they can hear the Lord more clearly when they get quiet.

Be still, and know that I am God (Psalm 46:10).

We have to see ourselves already in the Spirit as Christians.

So then they that are in the flesh cannot please God. **But ye are not in the flesh, but in the Spirit, if so be that the Spirit of**

God dwell in you. *Now if any man have not the Spirit of Christ, he is none of his*" (Romans 8:8-9).

As we are in Christ, we are in the Spirit. We just need to get our minds aligned to spiritual things.

In the place of prayer, we have to be spiritually minded. Tell your mind, "God wants to speak to me". Tell your mind, "My prayers avail much". Focus your mind on God's word and His promises. In the place of prayer, we have to be spiritually minded.

Have you found yourself in the place of prayer and suddenly remembered a person you want to send a WhatsApp message to? You send the message, only to find out that your message is still unread two days later. So, there is your evidence that the thought was a distraction. As mentioned above, a good idea is to have a pen and a small booklet you can write your thoughts on when they pop up during prayer. It will help your mind get quiet.

CHAPTER FIVE

YOUR MIND AND PRAYING IN THE SPIRIT

P raying in the Spirit is essential for every believer. The Lord has given us a secret weapon, i.e., our ability to pray in the Spirit.

Yes, we pray in our understanding, but we must also pray in the Spirit. Praying only in understanding, to be honest, will be a very limited prayer life because our minds cannot go past what we know. Only the Holy Spirit knows what exactly we should be praying about at any given time. As a matter of fact, praying in the Spirit is part of the armour we must put on.

Above all, taking the shield of faith, wherewith ye shall be able to quench all the fiery darts of the wicked. And take the helmet of salvation, and the sword of the Spirit, which is the word of God: **Praying always with all prayer and supplication in the Spirit,** *and watching thereunto with all perseverance and supplication for all saints* (Ephesians 6:16-18).

So, we can see that praying in the Spirit is essential for every believer. Praying in the Spirit is praying in tongues.

So, what happens when we pray in the Spirit?

For if I pray in an unknown tongue, my spirit prayeth, but my understanding is unfruitful (1 Corinthians 14:14).

When we pray in the Spirit, our spirit is praying but our minds are unfruitful.

For if I pray in tongues, my spirit is praying, but I don't understand what I am saying (1 Corinthians 14:14; NLT).

Because when we pray in the Spirit, we do not understand what we are saying. Our minds can hinder us if permitted. Your mind might be saying, "What is going on?" However, you need to tell our mind that "my spirit is praying". Don't allow your mind to kick you out of praying in the Spirit. You need to understand that your spirit is praying, and your understanding is unfruitful if you will stay in the place of prayer for a long time.

Praying in the Spirit is very effective, and we must be spiritually minded on this matter.

Chapter Six

YOUR MIND AND YOUR AFFECTIONS

Our affections are our passions, i.e., what drives us, and our priorities. Therefore, what we regularly think about will affect our passions and desires. The scriptures say, "For as he thinketh in his heart, so is he" (Proverbs 23:7).

What are you always thinking about? Can we see why our minds do matter in our Christian walk? This is why the Bible tells us what to think about.

Finally, brethren, whatsoever things are true, whatsoever things are honest, whatsoever things are just, whatsoever things are pure, whatsoever things are lovely, whatsoever things are of good report; if there be any virtue, and if there be any praise, think on these things (Philippians 4:8).

The Bible will not tell us what to think about if our thoughts are unimportant.

The scriptures tell us to set our affections on things above. You must be intentional in doing this.

If ye then be risen with Christ, seek those things which are above, where Christ sitteth on the right hand of God. Set your affection on things above, not on things on the earth. For ye are dead, and your life is hid with Christ in God" (Colossians 3:1-3).

*Since you have been raised to new life with Christ, set your sights on the realities of heaven, where Christ sits in the place of honor at God's right hand. **Think about the things of heaven, not the things of earth.** For you died to this life, and your real life is hidden with Christ in God"* (Colossians 3:1-3; NLT)

What are your predominant thoughts about?

This is part of renewing our minds. We must remember that what we see is temporal, and things that are not seen are eternal.

What are you looking at? What is your focus?

This explains why some Christians go to church on Sunday, and after that, it is till next week Sunday. During the week, you will not know that they are Christians. Once they are out of the church, their minds are set on the secular. Even if the Lord brought someone across their paths to minister to, they probably would not discern the opportunity.

While we look not at the things which are seen, but at the things which are not seen: for the things which are seen are temporal; but the things which are not seen are eternal (2 Corinthians 4:18).

Have you ever come across someone so passionate about the things of the Lord? This is partly what they have done. They have renewed their minds to the reality of spiritual things and fixed their gaze accordingly.

CHAPTER SEVEN

SHARING OUR FAITH

I once heard someone say, "Everyone is eternal". I don't think I will forget that phrase.

The truth is, every man is eternal. What does this mean? Every man will spend eternity somewhere.

It doesn't matter where they live, what neighbourhood they live in, how poor or wealthy they are; everyone needs to hear and respond to the gospel of our Lord Jesus Christ.

When you come across an opportunity to share your faith, don't allow your mind to deceive you. This is why we need to renew our minds. Listen to the Holy Spirit and yield to Him; refuse to be intimidated. Don't allow your mind to tell you, "Oh, the person is okay. They are doing well financially, can't you see their designer wears?" Eternity is real, and you might be the last person this individual might meet that will share the gospel with them.

Everyone needs to come to know the Lord Jesus Christ and receive the sacrifice He has paid for all men. This is another reason we need to be spiritually minded. It will be easier for us to discern when the Lord brings someone across our path to minister the glorious gospel to.

CHAPTER EIGHT

THE MIND OF CHRIST

The scriptures say that we have the mind of Christ (1 Corinthians 2:16). So, how do we apply this to our Christian walk?

To have the mind of Christ, we must see things the way the Lord sees things. This will be a process as we are all at different maturity levels. This means we have to renew our minds in the word of God. We need to see things the way the Lord sees things. Then, we have to adjust our mindsets to the heavenly realm.

Let us look at an example of a mindset of Jesus Christ our Lord.

Let nothing be done through strife or vainglory; **but in lowliness of mind** *let each esteem other better than themselves. Look not every man on his own things, but every man also on the things of others.* **Let this mind be in you, which was also in Christ Jesus:** *Who, being in the form of God, thought it not robbery to be equal with God: But made himself of no reputation, and took upon him the form of a servant, and was made in the likeness of men: And being found in fashion as a man, he humbled himself, and became obedient unto death, even the death of the cross. Wherefore God also hath highly exalted* *him, and given him a name which is above every name: That at the name of Jesus every knee should bow, of things in heaven, and things in earth, and things under the earth; And that every tongue should confess that Jesus Christ is Lord, to the glory of God the Father* (Philippians 2:3-11).

The above scriptures tell us that we are to put on the mindset of Christ. And in this case, the Bible is talking about humility.

Let us see verse 5 of Philippians 2 in other translations.

You must have the same attitude that Christ Jesus had (NLT).

*And consider the example that Jesus, the Anointed One, has set before us. Let his **mindset** become your motivation* (TPT).

So, from the above scriptures, we can see that our mindsets do play a vital role in our Christian walk,

*For this is the covenant that I will make with the house of Israel after those days, saith the Lord; **I will put my laws into their mind, and write them in their hearts:** and I will be to them a God, and they shall be to me a people* (Hebrews 8:10)

God's laws are not only in our hearts, but they are in our minds. Why are God's laws also in our minds? So we can align our thoughts and decisions to God's ways.

With God's laws in our minds and hearts, our thinking process should change. This is one reason we need to meditate on God's Word.

Chapter Nine

BEING SOBER-MINDED

As Christians, we need to be sober-minded.

What does it mean to be sober-minded? To take things seriously and refuse to be careless. Being sober is a weapon; it will cause a person to avoid certain things. Being sober-minded is also to be wise.

Be sober, be vigilant; because your adversary the devil, as a roaring lion, walketh about, seeking whom he may devour" (1 Peter 5:8)

In the Book of Titus, the Sripture tells young men to be sober-minded. We can also find in other parts of Scripture requiring us to be sober.

Young men likewise exhort to be sober minded (Titus 2:6).

In the same way, encourage the young men to live wisely (Titus 2:6; NLT)

In a similar way urge the young men to be sensible and self-controlled and to behave wisely [taking life seriously (Titus 2:6; AMP)

The things of God are serious, and the spirit realm is real. We have all been called to be sober (Titus 2:2; Titus 2:4; 1 Thessalonians 5:6).

The Book of Acts refers to the gospel as the words of truth and soberness.

But he said, I am not mad, most noble Festus; but speak forth the words of truth and soberness. (Acts 26:25).

A FOCUSED MIND

The scriptures say that a double-minded man is unstable in all his ways. Now, note that the Bible says he is unstable, not in some of his ways, but all his ways.

Our minds need to be focused on what is real, the truth of God, and His word.

This is why discipline comes in. We need to be careful what we feed our minds on, as this will affect our mindsets.

A double minded man is unstable in all his ways (James 1:8).

A person that wants to take their Christian walk seriously must have their minds focused on the things of the Lord. This is one measuring yard of people's commitment levels. A person with one foot in the world and one foot being a Christian is double-minded. Christ has paid a great price for us. We need to be fully committed to the Lord.

CHAPTER ELEVEN

THE COST OF BEING CARNALLY MINDED

We are all on a journey in renewing our minds. However, the scriptures tell us that we cannot afford to be carnally minded.

What does it mean to be carnally minded? A mind focused on the flesh, a mind that does not see things the way God sees things. A mind that is not spiritual.

For to be carnally minded is death; but to be spiritually minded is life and peace (Romans 8:6).

The above scripture speaks for itself.

Life and peace are products of a spiritual mind.

Because the carnal mind is enmity against God: for it is not subject to the law of God, neither indeed can be. So then they that are in the flesh cannot please God. But ye are not in the flesh, but in the Spirit, if so be that the Spirit of God dwell in you. Now if any man have not the Spirit of Christ, he is none of his (Romans 8:7-9).

The Bible further tells us that the carnal mind is enmity against God, and those in the flesh cannot please God. This is how important having a spiritual mind is.

The good news is that as Christians, we are not in the flesh but in the Spirit, according to Romans 8:9.

So, therefore, it is a matter of us following the instructions of Scripture for our minds.

Our minds need to be renewed by the Word of God.

Chapter Twelve
CONCLUSION

We have found out that our minds have a great role in our Christian walk.

Thank God that we have the greater one in us that has been sent to help us. The Holy Spirit, who is our helper (John 14:26).

Now that we have learnt the role our minds play in our Christian walk, let us get it to side with our spirits. This is done by renewing our minds by God's word.

Our minds need to side with what the Lord wants. We have been given everything that pertains to life and godliness (2 Peter 1:3). However, we must also remember that bringing every thought captive to the obedience of Christ is our responsibility.

We live in a world with so many distractions. This is the age that we cannot afford not to be spiritually minded in our everyday walk.

Thank God that His grace is sufficient for us.

SALVATION PRAYER

F ather God, I come to you in Jesus' name. I admit that I am a sinner, and I now receive the sacrifice that Jesus Christ paid for me.

I confess with my mouth the Lord Jesus, and I believe in my heart that God raised Him from the dead.

I now declare that Jesus Christ is my Lord and Saviour.

Thank you, Father, for saving me in Jesus' name.

I am now your child. Amen.

bisiwriter@outlook.com. Start reading your Bible and ask the Lord to guide you to a good church.

About the Author

B isi Oladipupo has been a Christian for many years and lives in the United Kingdom with her family.

Bisi attended a few Bible colleges, and she has completed a diploma in Biblical Studies from a UK Bible college.

She is a teacher of God's Word, coordinates Bible studies, and has a YouTube channel at

https://www.youtube.com/c/BisiOladipupo123.

She writes regularly, and her website is www.inspiredwords.org

Her author page is bisiwriter.com

bisiwriter@outlook.com.

QR Code for Bisi's Linktree:

ALSO BY BISI

The Twelve Apostles of Jesus Christ: Lessons We Can Learn

Believing on The Name of Jesus Christ: What Every
Believer Needs
to Know

Different Ways To Receive Healing From Scripture and
Walk in
Health

The Lord's Cup In Communion: The Significance of taking
the
Lord's Supper